L.I.F.E.

Learning to Initiate Forgiveness in Everything

Gilana Pearce

Contents

DEDICATION

For everyone who takes the time to read this book, this is dedicated to you as you go through life experiences of your own. Please know God is working everything out for your good.

I want to send a special dedication to Mary Epps, Mary Harper and my daddy, Maurice Harper, who always believed I could do anything.

ACKNOWLEDGEMENTS

To my husband, I thank you for being my rock, for loving me beyond myself at times and as Christ loves me. You are the epitome of selflessness, and I could never say thank you enough. To a very strong woman, my mommy, who taught me about God and the strength of a warrior. I salute you and your encouraging words every step of the way. Last, but definitely not least, to my children Desmic II and Ganiya, I am so proud to be called your mother. I expect greatness and pray I am a living example for you both in some way.

To every friend and every experience, I send a thank you note. To the experiences that taught me to love people past the surface level and to the ones who mistreated me, thank you as well. There was a lesson in it all, and I am grateful.

To my bishop and pastor who teach and train beyond themselves and love past all wrongs. I pray your strength to continue to live and be what God has called you to be.

INTRODUCTION

Who Am I?

I was about 36 years of age and had fallen into depression. I fell away from praying and reading like I was taught as a young person by my grandmother and my pastors from back home. I learned the hard way to never lose yourself trying to make a relationship or anything work. Only release things that won't prosper you, like bad attitudes, quick tempers, etc., but never relinquish the fiber of what makes you uniquely you. Depression is real and there is nothing wrong with Jesus and therapy (Christian therapy).

Do what you must to survive, push past stigmas and familiar opinions that don't benefit you. You know what you need, but don't be afraid to ask for help or reach out when you just need someone to listen. Have a strong friend in your corner for accountability to help you stay grounded and enable you to walk through this world in your truth.

It took a while for me to publish this book, but I am so grateful I did. I want to thank each and every one of you who will purchase or gift this work, and I pray you feel my heart through these life expressions. I hope this blesses you the way you need it to in this season of your life.

God bless you,
Gilana Pearce

A Mother's Love

Something intangible that touches every inch of your soul

Something that makes your incomplete days whole

It is strength when there is no one else to depend on.

Even the sound of her voice is a shoulder to lean on.

It encourages, disciplines and teaches in a special way

It guides and never leads you astray.

It's a mother's love.

A Soldier's Heart

You stood tall and proud

While the country cried aloud

For your safe return home to come soon

Maybe in the month of June.

We love you and thank you for your strength

Because it helps to protect us

Like a 1,000-foot fence.

Your courage we will never forget

Because we know the tough days aren't over yet.

Always put God first

Because He is the only one who can satisfy

Your first and last thirst.

No matter what you have done and said

God will always be your Daily Bread.

He is your secret strength from day to day

That's why I hope you didn't forget to pray today.

Know that whatever you did in the past

Remember trouble and hard times won't always last.

God will see you through every struggle and test

No matter what happens we thank God you did your best.

While you are being a soldier for Uncle Sam

Be a soldier for the "I am that I am."

Try to always keep God first it always works for me

Then you will always have peace

And know in your heart

You have the VICTORY!

A Sister's Love

A sister's love

Will protect like a mother.

A sister's love

Gives you the support you need.

A sister's love tells you

"Little brother, take heed."

A sister's love

Always looks out for you.

A sister's love

Encourages and prays you through.

What comes directly from above?

Nothing less

Than a sister's love.

Affections

The affections of a mate give encouragement to your soul.

Affections of a mate can naturally make and mold

Your relationship into a very beautiful thing.

Affections of a mate make winter feel like spring.

A husband's touch, a wife's kiss makes the whole world

Feel like a soothing mist.

Affections make your heart patter and your spirit jump.

Affections are sometimes hard to give

But affections can make a relationship

Die or live.

Beautiful

Hair not long enough

Teeth not straight

Better learn quick

How to appreciate yourself being beautiful in your own eyes

Never waiting on a man to determine the worth of your prize.

You are a strong woman stand tall and proud.

Let your humble presence make you unique in the crowd.

God sees you as something to be admired

So focus on God's will and your heart's desire.

Never live by anyone's standard of you

Only look to God and His directions to see you through.

Now that

Is

Beautiful

Don't Block My Flow

Don't tear her spirit help her keep her glow.

These are things to do so you won't block her flow.

She can build up and tear down with her hands.

Her wisdom is like a well of water flowing to no end.

Don't build a dam of negativity in her spirit to stop her flow.

She is equipped to carry burdens

You can't even begin to know.

She can handle just about anything that comes her way.

She's a Proverbs 31 woman for her family every day.

She endures all of this and the half has never been told.

Could you even imagine her force in the Kingdom

If you just unblocked her flow?

Brown Eyes

Deep and tender in spirit at a young age

Well beyond her years at her stage.

She looks at your spirit

To judge you first

And with her soft brown eyes

She decides if she can trust.

She looks up to Mommy and Daddy and tells us how she feels

And any worry that she has we do our best to heal.

They hold curiosity for this earthly place

We strive to teach her

One thing is to never look at race.

Never look at race as an asset or liability.

The world will do enough of that for you

Instead, look at race as a token of God's great masterpiece

So one day we will walk globally in the Master's peace.

Co-Pastor Deborah Dukes

Wise beyond your years

Eyes that see your soul

An anointed woman of God

Who helps you "Unblock Your Flow."

A co-pastor like no other

A straight-up talking spiritual mother

A woman who doesn't spare the spiritual rod

But instead rebukes you "Through the Eyes of God."

Someone who brings out the best in you

Even if the process is tough to go through.

She may make you shed some tears

But it will help you prosper in your latter years.

Married to a mighty man of God we see

And notice your relationship has a spirit of peace.

Your anointed voice captivates God's people in a unique way

So my request is for you to continue

To let God have His way.

God bless you and we love you!

Daddy

He has her back, is what she believes
His encouraging words put her at ease.
She falls asleep in his protecting arms
As he whispers to her, "I'll keep you from all harm."
"Daddy won't let anything happen to you," he says
As he teaches her to say her "Daily Bread."
He corrects her with a strong voice
To direct her to always make a wise choice.
Even though he whispers as he rocks her to sleep
There is another voice so soft but deep
She will have to listen to defeat
All other noise and voices that will try to lead her away
From a higher call and a purpose
That you placed inside her for such a time as this.
She will follow and let what was instilled lead her from within.

INTRODUCTION TO
DEATH IN THE TONGUE

I believe God gave me this gift of writing poetry as an outlet to reach women of all ages, but especially my young women who have gone through some things that just seem like they are not going to end. I wrote this poem to let you know that you can make it if you put your hand in God's hand. Some people use the excuse that they don't have a father, but I am a living testimony that God will pick you up and fulfill that lack that Daddy couldn't give you. I grew up without my biological father in the home. I knew him, but I didn't live with him. I grew up with a stepfather from around the age of twelve and had some hard times. I literally almost lost my mind in the midst of it, but I thank God for a Mom who told me to keep my mind stayed on Him who, of course, is the Father of all fathers.

Now I know God meant it for my good because today (twelve years later), I am writing this book to be a blessing to other women who have gone through hard times, whether verbal abuse or similar situations. If you don't remember anything else from this poem, know that you can make it through and God doesn't give you more than you can bear. Also, if He gives you the test, He can trust you to pass it.

Stay strong, endure as a good soldier and come out victorious!

Death in the Tongue

Harsh words hit you like a fist

Tear your spirit in so many ways

You want to number your days.

Words that birth all your fears

Words that give you nothing but tears

Words that make or break.

How can a tongue create so much hate?

Words that make you desire to renounce your days

But somehow that's not a factor when someone prays.

Words that make you yearn for nothing in life

Words that produce confusion and strife.

There is a way out, a King in the land who

Makes your heart shout.

Someone who knows every fear and wipes away every tear.

One who says

"Vengeance is mine"

And gives you joy for a lifetime.

He has purposed in you ministry

And gives you the strength to fulfill your destiny.

When someone speaks death to your destiny

Remember as far as you can see

That's how much

He'll expand your territory!

Duties of a Spouse

When I say "yes"

You say "no"

When I walk fast,

You walk slow.

When I see the enemy

You say "no way"

When I let it slide

There's a price to pay.

How hard is it to please

Your spouse and God

Without neglecting one

Or the other?

Thy rod and staff

They comfort me

In times of spiritual warfare

Commanding the devil to flee

Because you already have the victory.

The victory to walk upon serpents and cast away 10,000.

The duty is to cover, correct and love unconditionally.

Emotions

Am I taken seriously?

Do you know what I feel?

Are you truly in tune?

Do you know what is real?

Is this serious?

Are we on one accord?

Do you see the invisible discord?

We are one.

That's what God says

When we slack on reading our

Manna from Heaven.

It's up to us if we stand and continue to walk hand in hand.

Take my words to heart

Just like from the start

Take every word for its worth.

When our spouses speak

Let our spirits agree

To what each other needs

Before it's too late

Let's heed.

Faith

Untouchable

Unshakeable

Fully trusting in God.

Untouchable, unshakeable in whatsoever you ask.

As long as you stay diligent and obedient to your tasks

It can move mountains with only the size of a mustard seed.

Now tell me how much more you could achieve.

Now what about faith the size of a mountain?

Surely, He would pour out of His ever-flowing fountain.

Just like Abraham, God says, "As far as the eye can see."

I don't know about you

But that sounds better than that mustard seed to me.

Humbleness

Don't mistake it for low self-esteem, please!

It withstands and gives tolerance in the midst of a tease.

It enhances tolerance when you want to serve an attitude

But operating with humbleness advances your altitude.

You need true humbleness to do ministry

Because there are plenty of opportunities to abort your destiny

Through disobedience and prideful thoughts.

It is one of the toughest traits to carry

But is one of the most important when you marry.

Intimacy

Make love to my mind

When you look into my eyes

Whisper sweet nothings

To make my temperature rise.

Touch me in a way

That gives me chills.

As husband and wife

Never lose the thrill

Of being in each other's presence.

As king and queen

It can be difficult to maintain

But if you do

A healthy marriage is to gain.

Love

Something unexplainable, yet so hard to let go

A lack of it could definitely block your flow.

A holder of blessings and miracles in life

It casts out fear and deals with strife.

It mends old wounds and overcomes pain.

It can be difficult to withhold in true ministry.

After all, ministry is birthed from misery.

It will stand the test of time in everything you do.

Love is the strongest when it's tried and remains true.

Love Your Neighbor

Love your neighbor as yourself
Don't ever underestimate your inner wealth.

Always remember
You reap what you sow.

Treat everyone with genuine love and not for show.

Love your neighbor like God loves you.

You really learn love
When you are tried in the fire and come through.

Love your neighbor in spite of the disrespect you could receive.

Love your neighbor when you don't feel it
But always be watchful
God didn't make you stupid.

Obey God and you will always come out on top.

When you love sincerely
There's not a blessing anyone can stop.

Marriage

Marriage is sacred in every way.

You are designed not to defile the bed in which you lay.

It is a covenant that shouldn't be easily broken.

Understand your trials together when you are chosen.

It is what you make of it, you see.

As for the woman

Read Proverbs one plus thirty.

You are destined to be blessed if you hold steadfast without complaint.

Your true king's love will not hold any restraint.

He is designed to be the provider and strong head of the house

But only when he's in order with God can he truly lead his spouse.

He is the keeper and sensual lover of your soul.

He is the natural king meant to make you whole.

He is your strong tower

And his love on you should continually shower.

The most important thing to remember

When stepping into this commitment

Is to know that when arguments come

You can't call your parents to schedule an appointment.

He fights enough in the workplace and in the streets

When he comes home, there should be refuge in the sheets.

Marriage 2 of 2

It is a time of healing

Sharing all pain and wounds.

If you trust no one else

Your husband should be your best friend in time of gloom.

She can build up a house

Or tear it down with her hands.

And the wife should always know her position of prayer

Concerning her husband's plans.

She continuously gives him praise

And when she does

The more blessed are her days.

She is the natural keeper of his heart and soul

And what a "bad" woman she will be spiritually

When she realizes her words make him whole continuously.

From the inside out

She is the very essence of his being

Never speaking death in his spirit

And always being the virtuous woman.

And through tests

Enduring.

Mommy

A Mommy bears what her children can't take

She's the mender of broken hearts.

When her child makes mistakes

She has a way with her words

That can cut like a sword.

Her tongue gives sound rebuke

That comes straight from the Word.

Her steps are ordained by God.

I now know how

She gave the devil no glory

And refused to bow.

She refused to bow to the enemy's tactics

And what people put her through.

Her strength even today

Is tried and true.

She is a true model of

Virtue and strength to me.

Her children know

When she enters a room

The devil has got to flee.

That to me is a Mommy

That to me is my mommy.

My Seed

Intelligent, loving

In her own right.

Strong, independent

And willing to fight

For what she believes.

She stands strong

And in the time of trouble

She falls to her knees.

That's what I teach my seed.

Daughter, you are amazing, and I knew it the
day I laid eyes on you.

Don't hold grudges and don't walk in fear, but do walk in wisdom
and have a godly ear to His instructions and that feeling God
places in your gut.

Obedience

Obedience is better than sacrifice

That's what the Word says.

Why do we follow our path

When it's obviously not better than what He has?

We say we love Him

But slap Him in the face

When He tells us to go there

And willingly go another place.

We pray unceasingly about what we want in life

But never ceasing to see someone else blessed yet holding strife.

No matter how strong

His instructions are

Just endure as a good soldier

And your reward won't be far.

Being disobedient is never the thing to do.

If you think so

Your same trial

You'll continue to go through.

There's nothing better in the world to do for yourself

Because listening to Him gives you true wealth.

It seems so hard to hear His voice

But you have no problem listening to negative noise.

When you realize walking in obedience is the best place to be

It's a guarantee you'll find prosperity!

Practice What You Preach

Sometimes it's hard to practice what you preach.

Especially when it's someone close to you

Who gives you the speech.

It's not easy to grasp

No matter when it comes.

It makes it even harder

To hold your tongue.

So when it comes

Just take it

All in stride

Because if you don't

A fall comes right after pride.

Prayer

A main nutrient to a good life

What casts out strife

It talks directly to Abba

And produces in your life a moment of Shammah.

Responds to what you need

But only if you listen as His seed.

It can deliver, set free and heal.

When He directs your path in life

There's not a better deal.

It gives you instructions on things

You can't begin to understand.

It is literally your spiritual helping hand.

Rebuke

The hardest thing to do amongst friends

Wanting nothing more than conversation

God directs you to give them revelation

Concerning their life and things you see.

I am not telling you for my sake, trust me.

You give attitude from me being obedient.

But if you chose to listen

You would reap joy exceedingly.

I don't mind a good rebuke

If it will lead my soul to the truth.

The truth that lies within my soul

When I finally let God take control.

Release

Giving your all and nothing in return

Release

Sacrificing time, money and love

Release

Giving encouragement and understanding

Release

Giving opportunity and failure being chosen

People come and go

Out of your life

Release

But when it's ministry

You have to understand maturity

Doesn't come with age.

Nor let blindness by the enemy

Lead you to rage.

When you've done and given all you can

There's truly nothing left to do but stand

On the promises and Word of God

To continue to be thy staff and rod.

When you make preparations for someone to increase

And their response is to make all positive choices cease

Then the very last thing to do is let go and let God and then finally

Release.

INTRODUCTION
TO SOLD OUT

This poem means a lot to me because it describes me. I grew up in church but didn't really give my life to God until I was about eleven or twelve years old. That's when God started giving me vivid dreams and visions of things before they happened, and I started to truly realize that I had a calling on my life.

This poem symbolizes being able to testify to anyone that they can stay sold out and keep themselves until marriage if they choose. Of course, it's not always easy, and yes, you have to stay in God's word for strength. I know many times young people think, If I don't give them any, they'll leave. Sweetheart, let me tell you something: The king or queen who is supposed to have your heart will wait until they say, "I do."

I'm not just telling you something I think, I can personally tell you first-hand that it is true. I was obedient to God and He sent me a king at a young age. The funny thing is we met as soon as I started going through tests and trials when I was twelve and he was thirteen. Ladies, I know the parents are probably saying, "That is a young age," but understand our so-called dates at twelve and thirteen were to Bible study, Prayer service, Tarrying service and Sunday worship. We were taught that's where you start and if you're serious about it, everything else will come to pass.

I am here to be real. Yes, your flesh feels emotions and would like to do things, but you have "to know that you know" where all your blessings come from and remember this:

Whatever you put before God, is your God.

Sold Out

If you meet me and expect something more than friends

Just know that I'm sold out to the very end.

If you tell me you love me and think I'll put out

Let me make this loud and clear

I thought I told you I was SOLD OUT!

To all my ladies, it is possible to wait.

After all, isn't it worth it to make it through

Those Golden Gates?

Your price is far beyond rubies and gems

So, it is a personal choice

To keep your mind stayed on Him.

No short-term pleasure is worth my soul in a burning hell

Or to make my heavenly Father feel betrayal.

I know it is possible, I did it myself.

And I know if a man can't respect that

He could never deserve your

True wealth.

So never think you have to put out.

Instead look at all your riches

If you just stay

SOLD OUT.

The Gift

You may think I'm stuck up

With a nasty attitude.

I am very straightforward

You may think I'm rude.

When you meet me

Right from the start

You quickly find out

My body is a temple

And you gets no parts.

It was designed for my king

And no one else.

So when I say, "I do"

I know he'll get the very best.

Something so special, no one has ever had.

In this case, my husband will receive

My first and last.

What is it you ask?

It's the Gift.

Time

It comes and goes quickly

How much is it worth?

Is it valuable enough to celebrate His birth?

How will you spend it today?

Will you have enough time to pray?

What about lifting your brother up

Not even knowing your words could change his strut?

Do you have it to encourage that sister down the street?

Or will you say,

"I didn't have time"

When you hear of her last heartbeat?

Do you have enough time to call Jesus by His name?

Or when you need Him, will He be ashamed?

Will you spend it selfishly

Never fully knowing the Trinity?

Oops, out of time....

The crazy thing is that regardless of when this poem was written,

It is still current and relevant.

Ignorance

When will we lose it?

When will it disappear?

Something that has no meaning

But yet as sincere.

How it easily comes and goes

In the homes and workplace.

Yet the main ones that do it

Can't look you in the face.

It's disgraceful, distasteful

Yet everyone wants a taste.

All you end up getting is your time wasted.

You can ignore it

Cover it up

Or even bury it.

The only way it will stop

Is if people stop sharing it.

Wake up

Grow up

Educate the youth.

Give them a real sense of being

And strong grounded roots.

Be an example

Stand tall and strong.

Endure as good soldiers and put ignorance

Where it belongs.

Rely on no one to make a difference but you.

The only thing that's going to matter

Is the decision you choose.

The person you decide to portray

Depends on whether you win or lose.

Time is of the essence

This is true.

Infecting other people,

It's totally up to you.

ABOUT THE AUTHOR

As a shy southern country girl born in Tarboro, NC but raised in Rocky Mount, NC, I have always had big dreams. I have always been determined to not just survive, but *thrive*. This ambition has taken me out of my comfort zone and into areas I never imagined. As a mother of two, wife, entrepreneur of multiple businesses, and now author, I am living my best life. This composition has been years in the making. If you read the synopsis, you can understand why it took me so long to publish. This is just the start of many more books I plan to produce in the future. The many challenges I have had to overcome. The countless experiences I have endured. The endless trials I continue to face and overcome all come together to create the woman of God represented here. I continue to learn, grow, and develop myself as life's situations and outcomes mold my being into a woman of power and influence. I sincerely thank you for taking the time to invest in me. I have poured my heart and soul into these poems and hopefully you are able to see my product as an investment in you.